RECORD BREAKERS

RECORD-BREAKING
PEOPLE

DANIEL GILPIN

PowerKiDS
press™

New York

Published in 2012 by The Rosen Publishing Group Inc.
29 East 21st Street, New York, NY 10010

Copyright © 2012 Wayland/
The Rosen Publishing Group, Inc.

First Edition

Senior Editor: Debbie Foy
Designer: Rob Walster
Picture Researcher: Kate Lockley

Library of Congress Cataloging-in-Publication Data

Gilpin, Daniel.
Record-breaking people / by Daniel Gilpin. -- 1st ed.
    p. cm. -- (Record breakers)
Includes index.
ISBN 978-1-4488-5293-2 (library binding)
1. Sports records--Juvenile literature. 2. Athletes--Biography--Juvenile literature. I. Title.
GV741.G55 2012
796.02'1--dc22

                    2010047280

Manufactured in China
CPSIA Compliance Information: Batch # WAS1102PK: For Further Information
contact Rosen Publishing, New York, New York at 1-800-237-9932

Photographs:

Holly Allen/Rex Features: 18 (inset)
© Toby Armstrong: 21
Barry Bland/Barcroft Media 22 (inset)
GERO BRELOER/epa/Corbis: 12
© Thomas Gregory: 14–15
Austin Hargrave/Barcroft Media/Getty Images: 9
iStockphoto/Rafal Belzowski: 24–25
JOE KLAMAR/AFP/Getty Images: COVER, 13
© Joar E. M. Klette: 10–11
Kim Komenich/San Francisco Chronicle: 27
Hiroyuki Kuraoka/AP/Press Association
    Images: 25 (inset)
Robert Kwiatek/Rex Features: 4
ALADIN ABDEL NABY/Reuters/Corbis: 22–23
NASA-JSC: 28–29
Phil Rees/Rex Features: 18–19
RIA Novosti/TopFoto/TopFoto.co.uk: 29(inset)
sharky/Alamy: 16–17
Sipa Press/Rex Features: 24, 26
Shutterstock: 20
Darren Taylor aka Professor Splash: 6–7
© David Weichenberger: 8, 30
AHMAD YUSNI/AFP/Getty Images: 5

Abbreviations used:

in. = inches
cm = centimeters
ft. = feet
m = meters
lb. = pounds
km = kilometers
kg = kilograms
mph = miles per hour
km/h = kilometers per hour

Tricky words are listed in "But What Does That Mean?" on page 31.

WHAT'S INSIDE?

MARIUSZ PUDZIANOWSKI

Meet Mariusz Pudzianowski, the world's strongest man. He has also won the World's Strongest Man competition a record-breaking five times!

Can You Believe It?

The competition's events include the "Plane Pull," where contestants pull an airplane along, and the "Car Walk," where contestants aim to carry a car as far as they can!

The world's strongest man takes part in the Plane Pull event.

WOW!

THE STRONG MAN EATS A LOT TO KEEP HIS WEIGHT UP. BREAKFAST INCLUDES 10 EGGS AND AROUND 2 LB. (1 KG) OF BACON. BETWEEN MEALS HE EATS CHOCOLATE AND OTHER SWEETS FOR ENERGY.

In this event, contestants walk as far as they can carrying heavy steel weights.

DARREN TAYLOR

Better known to his fans as Professor Splash, daredevil Darren Taylor holds the record for the world's highest dive into a shallow pool!

Can You Believe It?

Darren tours the world with his death-defying act and has broken his own world record several times. His high dive record currently stands at over 35 ft. (10.87 m)!

HIGHEST SHALLOW DIVE!

WOW!

FOR HIS INCREDIBLE RECORD-BREAKING JUMP, DARREN LEAPT FROM A SPECIALLY BUILT TOWER INTO A CHILDREN'S WADING POOL FILLED WITH JUST 12 IN. (30 CM) OF WATER!

Darren Taylor leaps from the tower—heading for the wading pool below!

DAVID WEICHENBERGER

On September 16, 2006, Austrian David Weichenberger jumped an amazing, record-breaking 9 ft. 8 in. (2.95 m) on his unicycle!

David's racing unicycle has heavy-duty tires, great for leaps and jumps!

Can You Believe It?

He uses his unicycle for racing as well as jumping. In 2008, David won the gold medal for downhill racing at the Unicycle World Championships in Denmark.

LONGEST UNICYCLE JUMP!

FRED GRZYBOWSKI

American thrill-seeker Fred Grzybowski holds the record for the world's highest pogo stick jump. In August 2007, he sprang 7 ft. 6 in. (2.28 m) from the ground!

Can You Believe It?

Fred makes a living as a professional performer, doing amazing pogo stick stunts at events all over the United States.

Fred also holds the world record for the most pogo stick backflips—a total of nine in a row!

9

CHRISTIAN SCHOU

Christian Schou from Norway is the record holder for the world's highest slackline walk. He made this amazing crossing on August 3, 2006.

Can You Believe It?

Christian's slackline was suspended 3,280 ft. (1,000 m) above ground, crossing a large cliff chasm. It was the same height as three Eiffel Towers!

Christian made his crossing barefoot and had a safety wire in case he fell.

HIGHEST SLACKLINE WALK!

WOW!

A SLACKLINE IS A FORM OF TIGHTROPE, BUT IT IS NOT PULLED TAUT ACROSS A GAP. INSTEAD, IT IS STRETCHY AND BOUNCY, LIKE A LONG, THIN TRAMPOLINE. THIS ALLOWS PEOPLE TO PERFORM AMAZING STUNTS AND TRICKS!

USAIN BOLT

FASTEST!

Usain Bolt is the world's fastest man. On August 16, 2009, he set a new 100-meter sprint world record of 9.58 seconds, running at an average speed 23 miles (37.58 km) per hour!

Can You Believe It?

Usain first broke the world record on May 31, 2008, and then again on August 16, 2009. He broke it for the third time three days later!

WOW!

USAIN'S 100-METER RECORD MAKES HIM 0.16 SECONDS FASTER THAN HIS NEAREST RIVAL, ASAFA POWELL, ANOTHER SPRINTER FROM JAMAICA.

Usain Bolt celebrates winning a gold medal for Jamaica in the 2008 Beijing Olympics.

Usain's nickname is "Lightning Bolt" because of his power on the track!

CONTENDERS

Usain Bolt is the world's fastest sprinter but Haile Gebrselassie from Ethiopia is the quickest long-distance runner. He finished a marathon in 2 hours, 3 minutes, and 59 seconds!

THOMAS GREGORY

On September 6, 1988, Thomas Gregory became the youngest person ever to swim the English Channel. He was just 11 years and 11 months old!

Can You Believe It?

To cross the Channel from the UK, Thomas had to swim 21 miles (34 km). He made the trip in just 11 hours and 54 minutes.

Thomas on his cross-Channel swim.

14

WOW!

LONG-DISTANCE SWIMMER ALISON STREETER HAS SWUM THE ENGLISH CHANNEL A RECORD-BREAKING 43 TIMES. IN 1990, SHE EVEN DID A NONSTOP CHANNEL CROSSING—THREE TIMES!

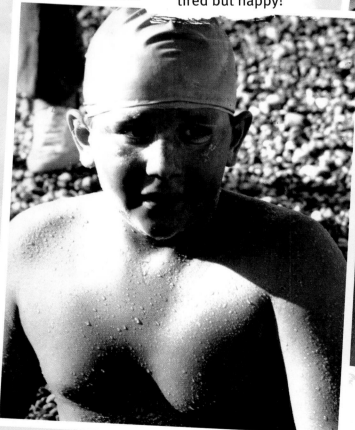

Thomas arrives on the shore in France, tired but happy!

Thomas's supporters congratulate him as he recovers from his long swim!

HERBERT NITSCH

Herbert Nitsch holds the record for the world's deepest free dive. In free diving, the diver has no breathing equipment—but must hold his or her breath!

Can You Believe It?

The Austrian dived to a depth of 702 ft. (214 m) on June 14, 2007. He went down with the help of a weighted sled, and then floated back to the surface with a "lifting bag" device.

Herbert dives deep into the ocean with the help of a weighted sled.

WOW!

STÉPHANE MIFSUD BROKE THE WORLD RECORD FOR HOLDING HIS BREATH UNDERWATER IN A SWIMMING POOL. THE FRENCHMAN HELD HIS BREATH FOR AN AMAZING 11 MINUTES AND 35 SECONDS!

Herbert rises to the surface after his dive.

DAVE CORNTHWAITE

On January 22, 2007, British adventurer Dave Cornthwaite rode an incredible 3,618 miles (5,823 km) across Australia on his skateboard!

Can You Believe It?

Dave took almost five months to make his journey across Australia. On the way, he went through 13 pairs of shoes, had a road race with a wild emu, and suffered lots of blisters!

On the road, in the middle of the Australian desert!

WOW!

DAVE SKATED FOR AN AVERAGE OF 30 MILES (48 KM) A DAY AND REACHED SPEEDS OF UP TO 30 MPH (48 KM/H) ON DOWNHILL RUNS!

Dave's skateboard was designed specially for the trip, with mudguards and a lower deck than normal!

RONALDO

Brazilian soccer player Ronaldo Luís Nazário de Lima has scored 15 World Cup goals—more than any other soccer player in the world!

MOST WORLD CUP GOALS!

Can You Believe It?

Ronaldo has played for Brazil in four World Cup tournaments—1994, 1998, 2002, and 2006. In 2002, he was Brazil's captain and scored both goals in the final, beating Germany 2–0.

WOW!

RONALDO HAS ALSO SCORED THREE OR MORE GOALS IN THREE DIFFERENT WORLD CUPS. THE ONLY OTHER PLAYER TO DO THIS IS GERMANY'S JÜRGEN KLINSMANN.

ALIA SABUR

Not many university professors are younger than their students! Alia Sabur was just 18 years and 362 days old when she became professor at Konkuk University in Seoul, Korea.

Can You Believe It?

Alia was reading by eight months old. She went to college at the age of ten, and had a degree in math by the time she was 14!

WOW!

ALIA'S TALENTS GO FAR BEYOND HER AMAZING BRAIN. AT NINE YEARS OLD, ALIA BECAME A BLACK BELT IN TAE KWON DO.

ASHRITA FURMAN

Record-breaking fanatic Ashrita Furman has set more records than anyone else in the world. Since 1979, he has set 283 records!

Can You Believe It?

In 1979, Ashrita set his very first world record by doing 27,000 star jumps. It was such a thrill, that Ashrita has not stopped since!

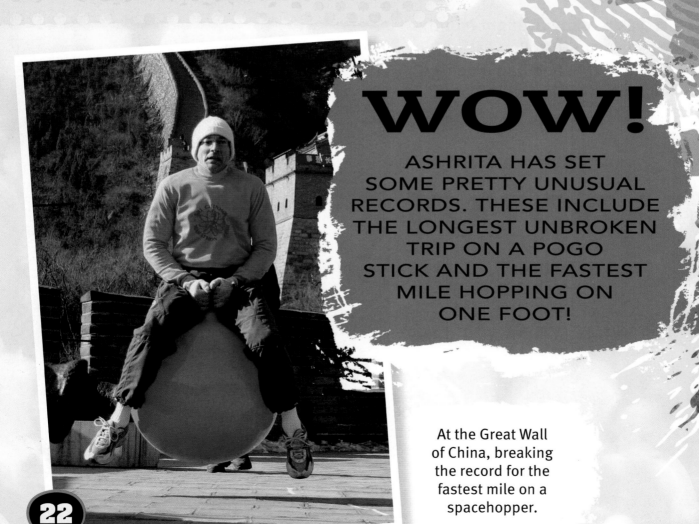

WOW!

ASHRITA HAS SET SOME PRETTY UNUSUAL RECORDS. THESE INCLUDE THE LONGEST UNBROKEN TRIP ON A POGO STICK AND THE FASTEST MILE HOPPING ON ONE FOOT!

At the Great Wall of China, breaking the record for the fastest mile on a spacehopper.

Ashrita attempting the record for the longest distance balancing a pool cue on one finger!

JORDAN ROMERO

On May 22, 2010, Jordan Romero from California became the youngest person ever to climb Mount Everest. At the time, he was just 13 years old!

Can You Believe It?

At the age of 10, Jordan climbed Mount Kilimanjaro in Tanzania. He wants to be the youngest person to climb the highest mountain on every continent!

WOW!

OVER 175 PEOPLE HAVE DIED TRYING TO REACH THE SUMMIT OF EVEREST. SADLY, MANY OF THEIR BODIES STILL LIE ON THE MOUNTAIN.

After his climb, Jordan said: "Standing on top of the world is the best feeling you could ever imagine."

24

On the Other Hand...

On May 22, 2007, a retired teacher from Japan became the oldest person ever to climb Mount Everest. When he reached the summit, Katsusuke Yanagisawa was 71 years and 61 days old!

Everest base camp, where climbers rest at the foot of the mountain.

JEANNE LOUISE CALMENT

Jeanne Louise Calment was the longest-living person on record. She was born in 1875 in Arles, France, and died in 1997 at the age of 122!

CONTENDERS

The world's oldest person living today is Eugenie Blanchard, who is also from France. She was born on February 16, 1896.

Can You Believe It?

Jeanne Louise Calment (pictured here) was old enough to remember the Eiffel Tower in Paris being built.

26

MARK ZUCKERBERG

Mark Zuckerberg is the founder and CEO of Facebook, and the world's youngest self-made U.S. dollar billionaire!

Can You Believe It?

In 2003, Mark was an ordinary student at Harvard University. In February 2004, he founded Facebook and today, he is one of the richest men in the world.

WOW!

MARK ZUCKERBERG WAS JUST 23 YEARS AND 296 DAYS OLD WHEN HE BECAME A BILLIONAIRE!

VALERI POLYAKOV

The longest unbroken space flight ever made was by the Russian cosmonaut, Valeri Polyakov.

Can You Believe It?

During 1994 and 1995, Polyakov spent an incredible 437 days orbiting the Earth aboard the Mir Space Station!

Valeri Polyakov seated in the Mir Space Station.

WOW!

MIR SPACE STATION WAS ABANDONED IN 2000. IT FELL BACK TO EARTH ON MARCH 23, 2001, BREAKING UP AS IT RE-ENTERED THE ATMOSPHERE. ITS UNBURNED PARTS CRASHED INTO THE PACIFIC OCEAN!

Though he has now retired
from space flight, Valeri still
works as a medical doctor.

CONTENDERS

Although Polyakov made the longest
single flight, Sergei Krikalyov has spent
more time in space than anybody else,
with a record of 803 days!

TEST YOURSELF!

Can you remember facts about the record-breaking people in this book? Test yourself here by answering these questions!

1. What was the name of the space station on which Valeri Polyakov made his record-breaking stay?

2. How old was Thomas Gregory when he swam the English Channel?

3. How many times has Mariusz Pudzianowski won the World's Strongest Man competition?

4. Which country is home to the world's fastest man?

5. Which social networking site was set up by Mark Zuckerberg, the world's youngest self-made billionaire?

6. How deep was the pool that Darren Taylor jumped into when he set his shallow dive world record?

7. How old was the world's oldest person ever when she died?

8. Which country did Dave Cornthwaite skateboard across to set his world record?

9. In which year did Ashrita Furman set his first world record?

10. How long was David Weichenberger's unicycle jump?

Answers

1. Mir
2. 11 years and 11 months old
3. 5 times
4. Jamaica
5. Facebook
6. 12 in. (30 cm)
7. 122
8. Australia
9. 1979
10. 9 ft. 8 in. (2.95 m)

BUT WHAT DOES THAT MEAN?

atmosphere   The layer of gas that surrounds the Earth.

backflip   A backward somersault in the air.

chasm   A deep opening in an area of rocks or cliffs.

CEO   This means Chief Executive Officer of a company or business.

contestant   A person who takes part in a competition.

cosmonaut   An astronaut from Russia or the former Soviet Union.

daredevil   A person who enjoys doing dangerous things.

English Channel   The stretch of sea between England and France.

fanatic   A person who is devoted to an activity or hobby.

marathon   A running race of 26 miles 385 yards (42.195 km).

orbiting   Circling, or flying around, another object

somersault   Turning head over heels in the air, and landing on your feet.

sprinter   A person who runs fast over short distances.

star jumps   An exercise that involves jumping in the air with arms and legs apart in a star shape.

stunt   A daring and difficult trick or move.

summit   The very highest point of a mountain.

suspended   To hang in the air.

tae kwon do   A Korean martial art, similar to karate.

taut   When something is pulled tight.

thrill-seeker   A person who enjoys doing dangerous things for fun.

tournament   A large sports competition with lots of competitors or teams.

unicycle   A type of bicycle that only has one wheel.

FURTHER INFORMATION, WEB SITES, AND INDEX

Places to go

Madame Tussauds
This world famous wax museum can be found in cities all over the world and features many interesting "people" from past and present.

Ripley's Believe It Or Not!
This exhibition can be found in different cities all over the world and has weird and wonderful things to see, including a model of the tallest man who ever lived!

Books to read

Guinness World Records, 2011
(Guinness World Records, 2010)

Ripley's Special Edition, 2011
(Scholastic Inc, 2010)

Web Sites

Due to the changing nature of Internet links, PowerKids Press has developed an online list of Web sites related to the subject of this book. This site is updated regularly. Please use this link to access this list:
http://www.powerkidslinks.com/record/people/

Index